# KITTENS
# ADORABLE

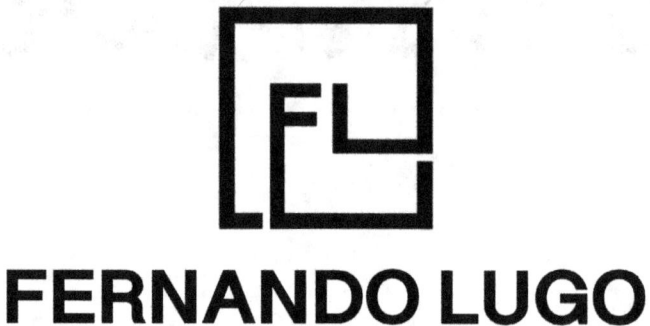

**FERNANDO LUGO**

# Kittens Will
## Conquer Your heart

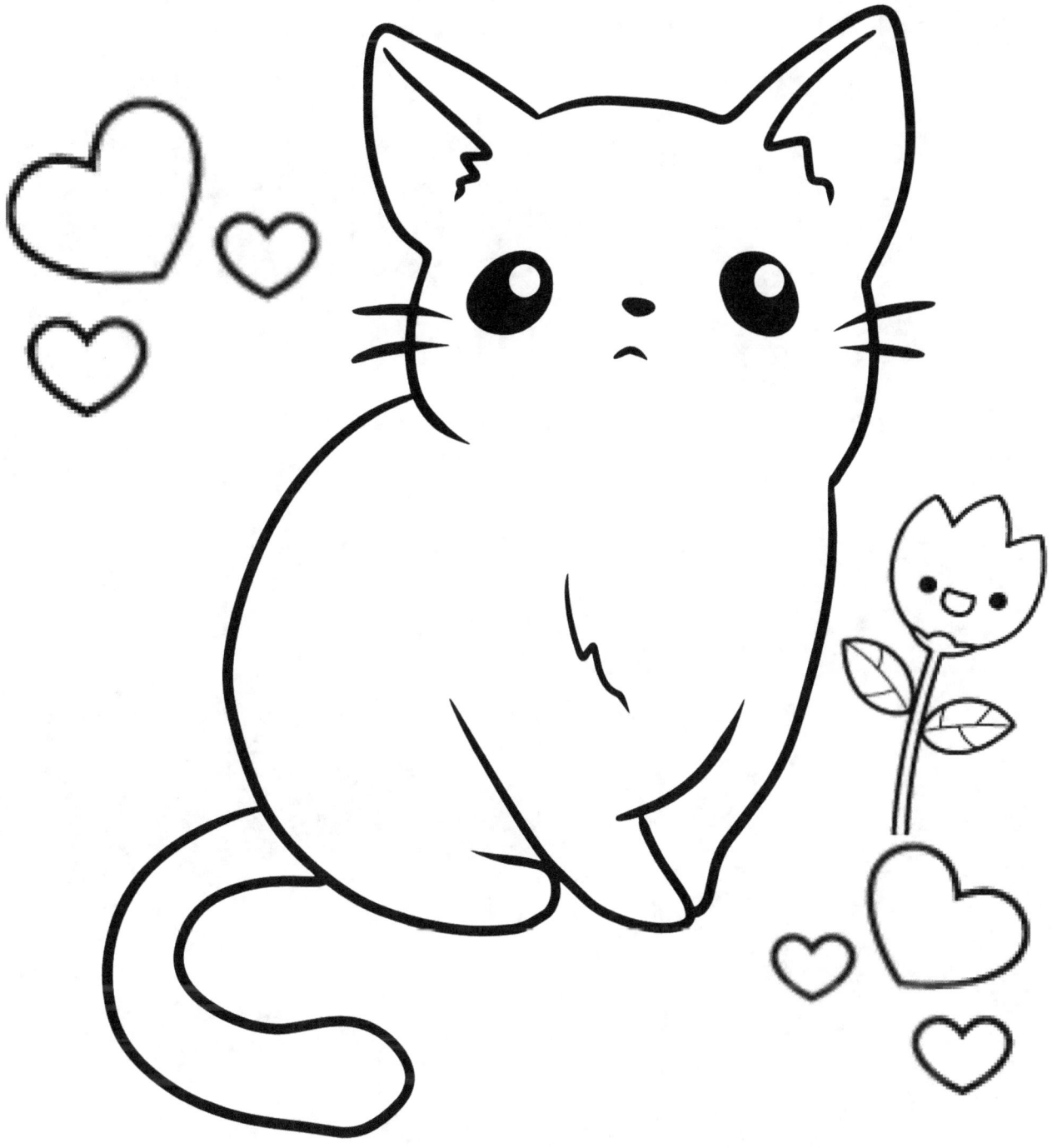

# Kittens Filled with Joy
## Every Corner

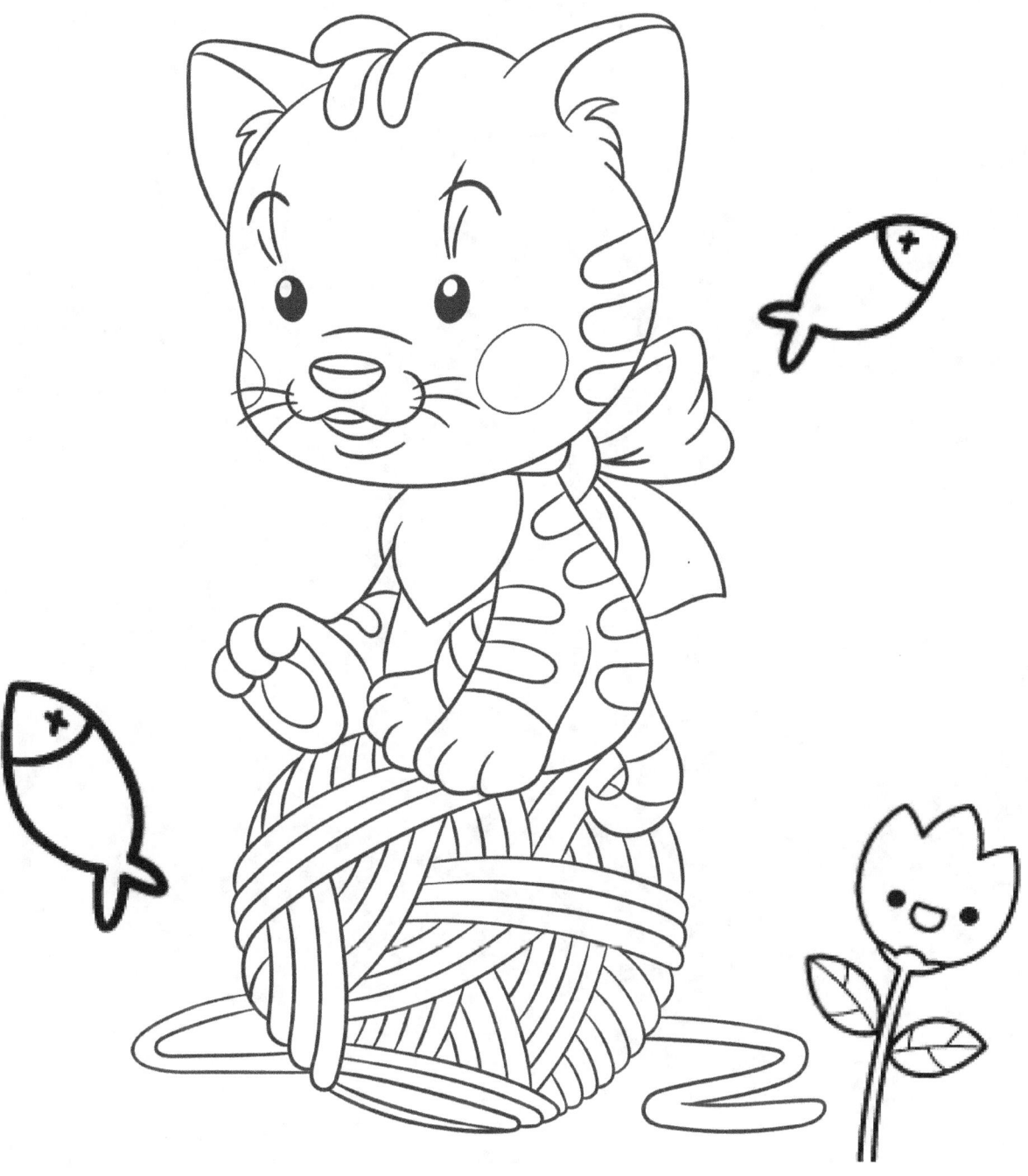

# Magic Garden

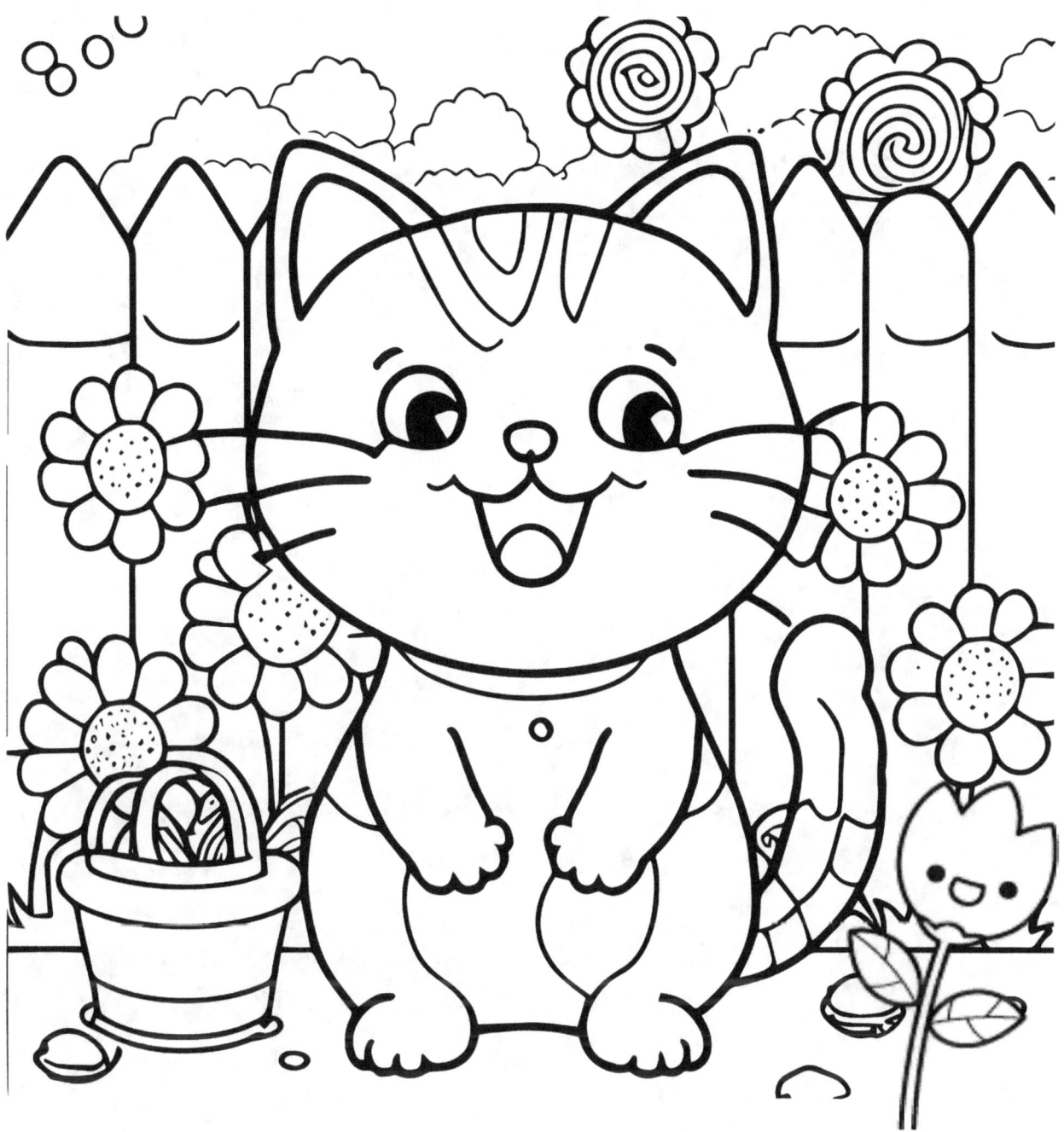

# I'm delighted

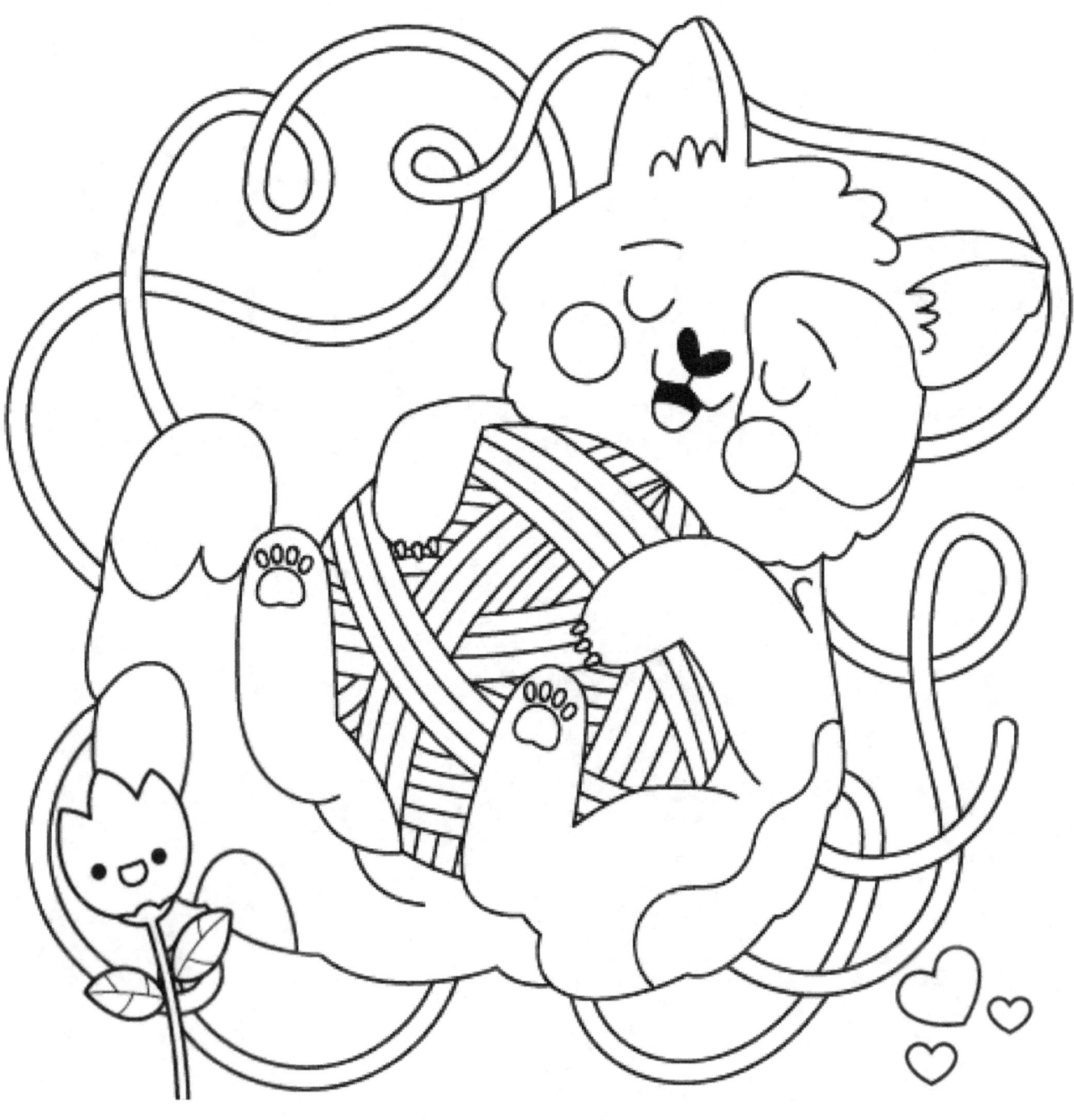

# In their Feline World, Cats
# They are kings and queens

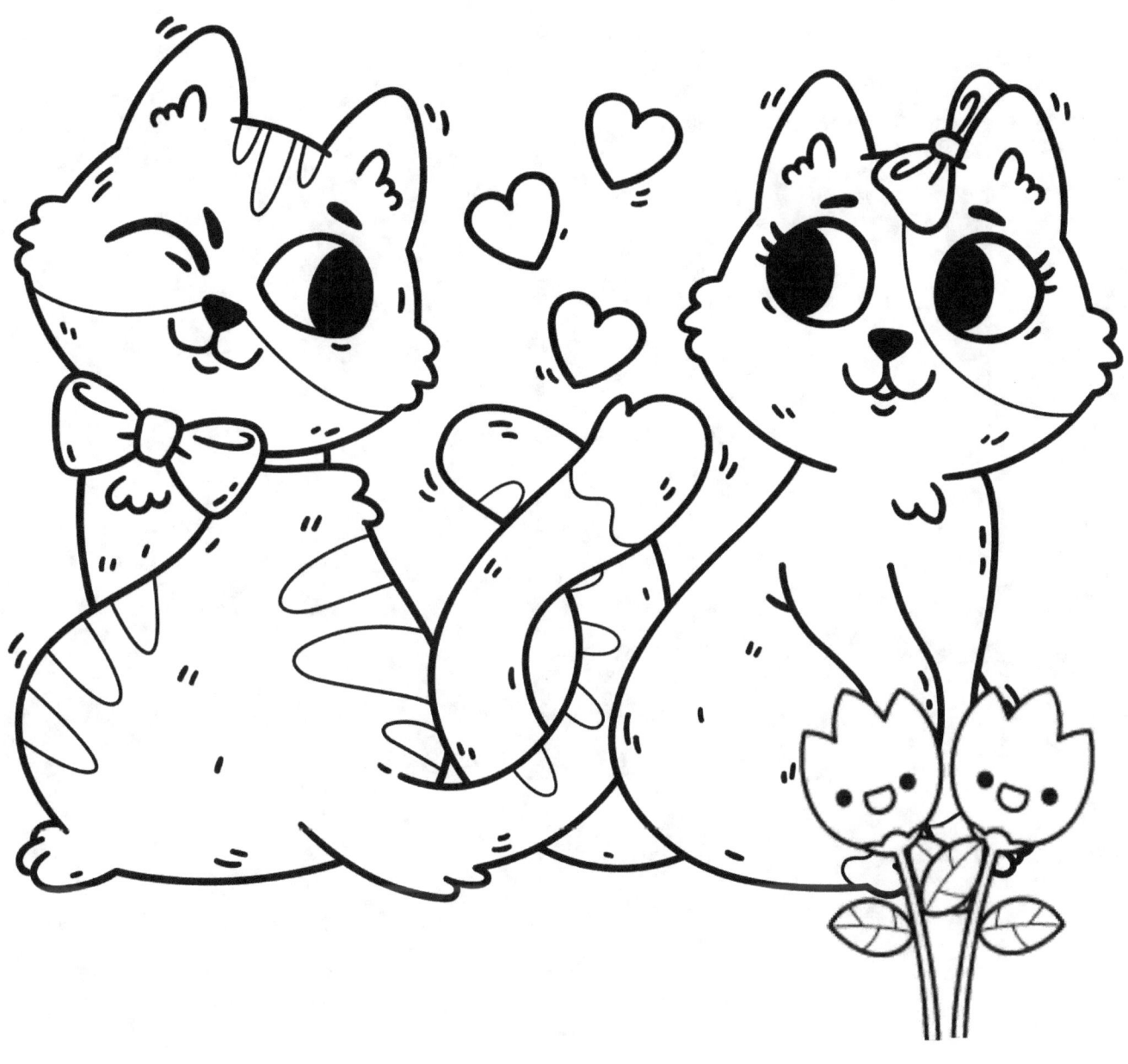

# I'm big

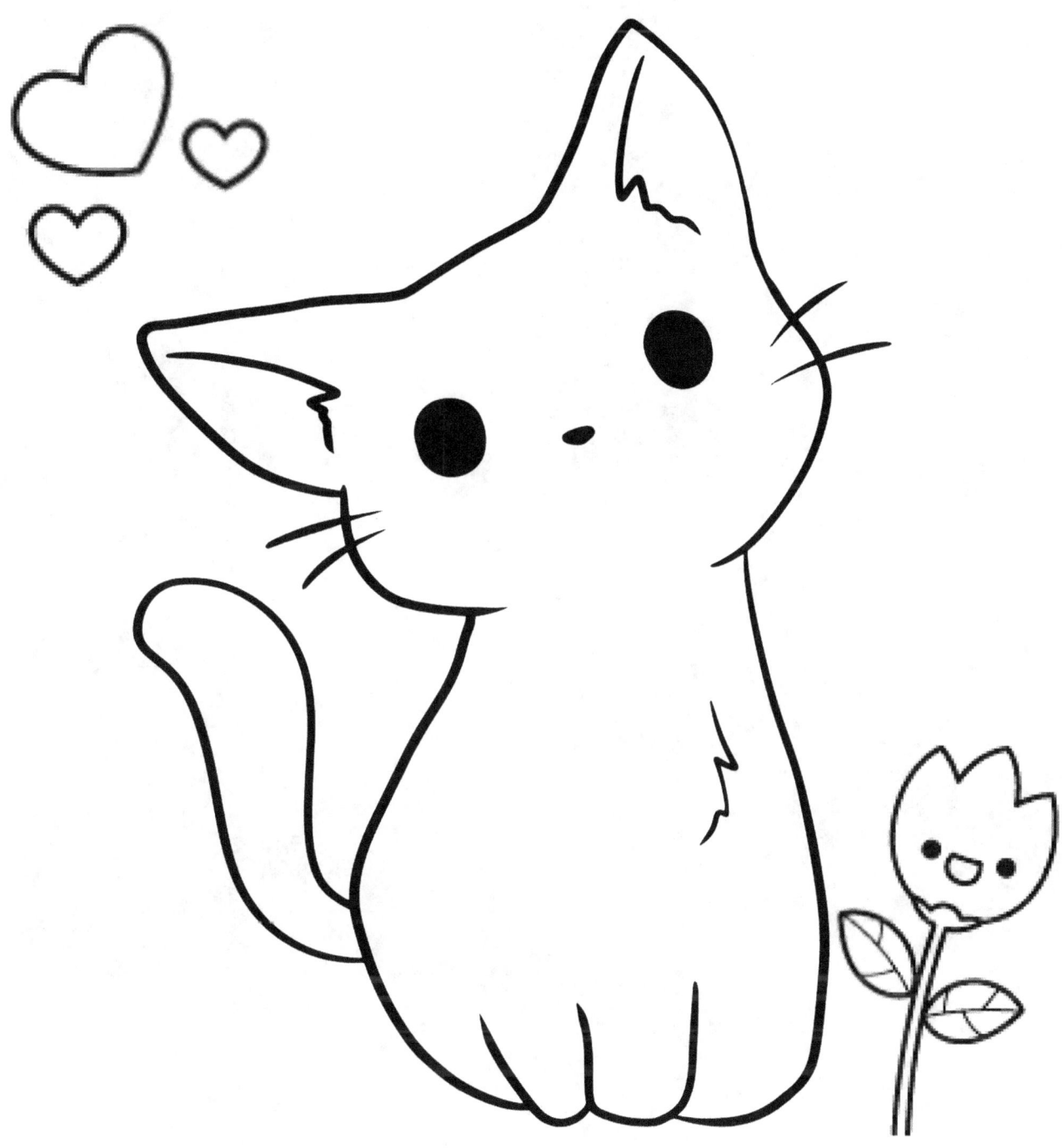

# That's lovely!

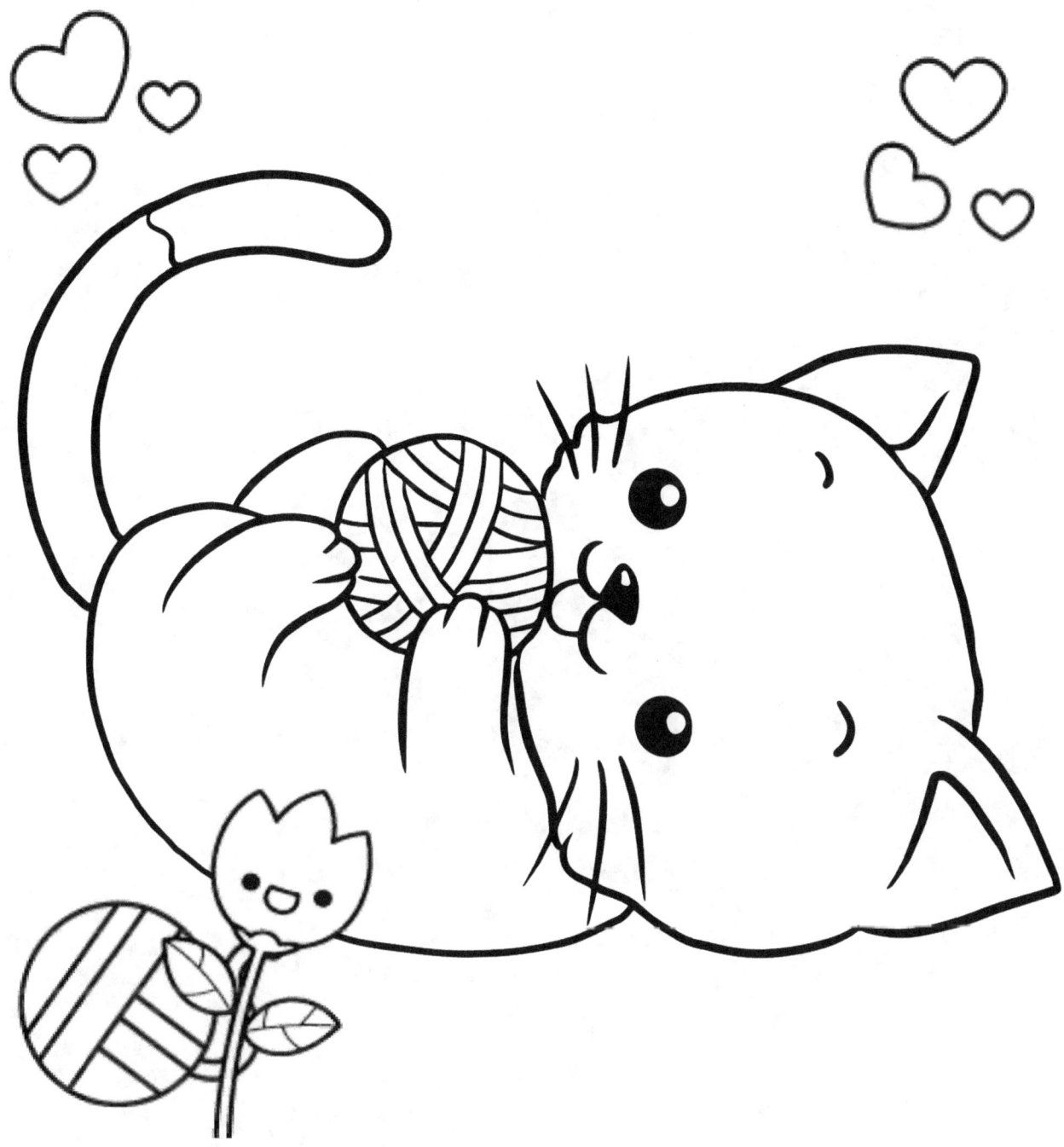

# Kittens Explore A world full of fun

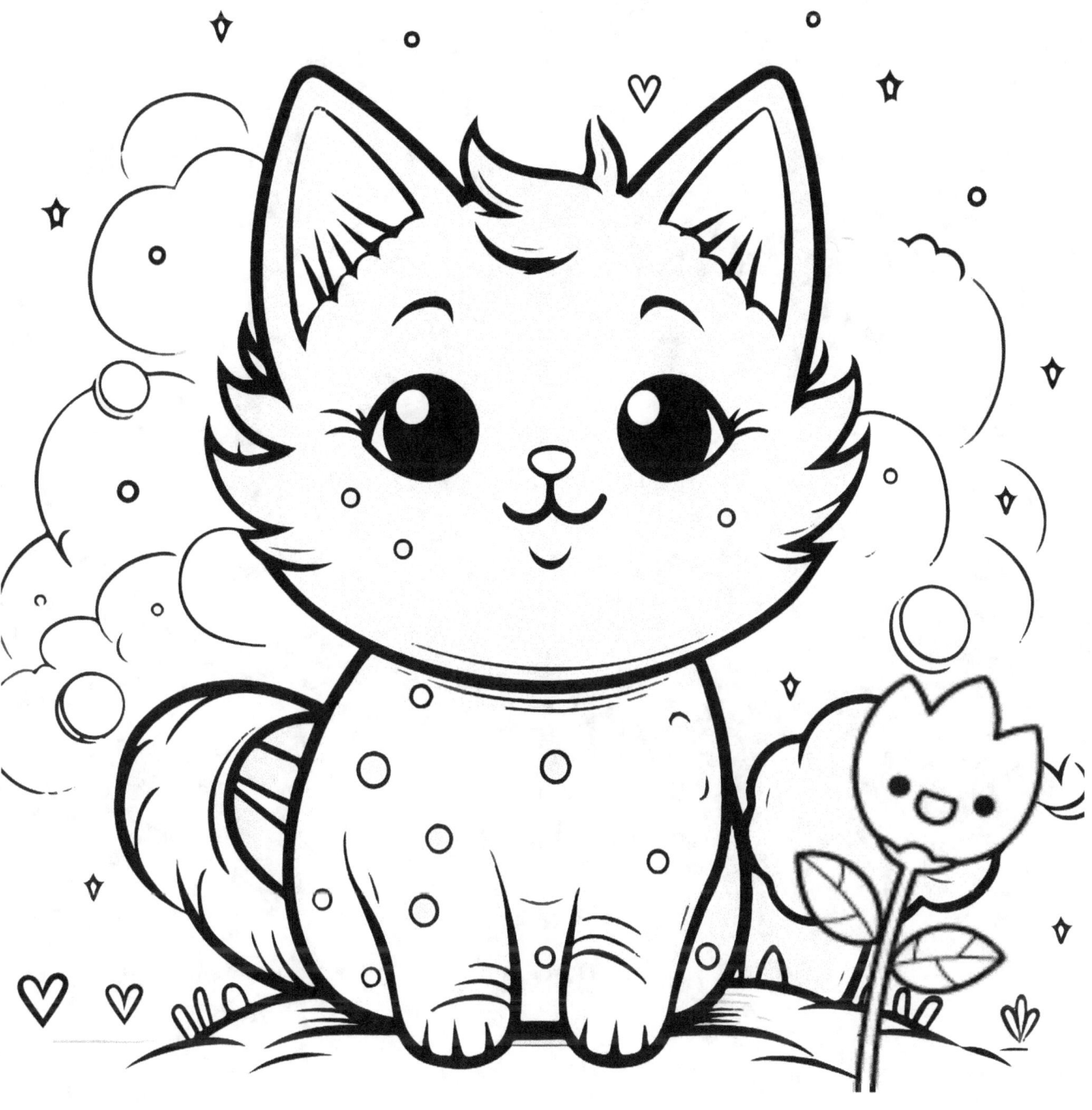

# Trip to the moon

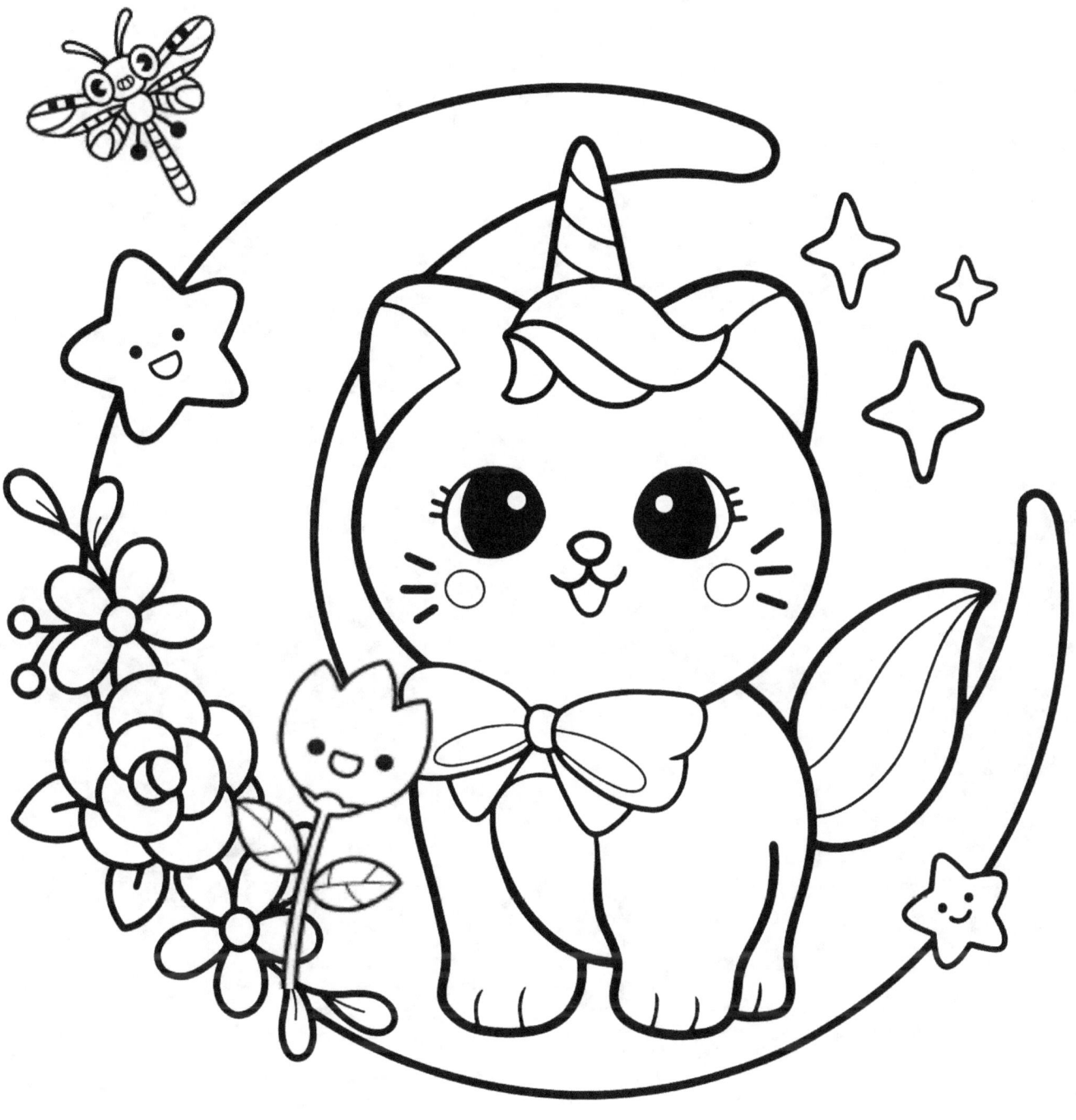

# Curious Cats Always You will find something interesting

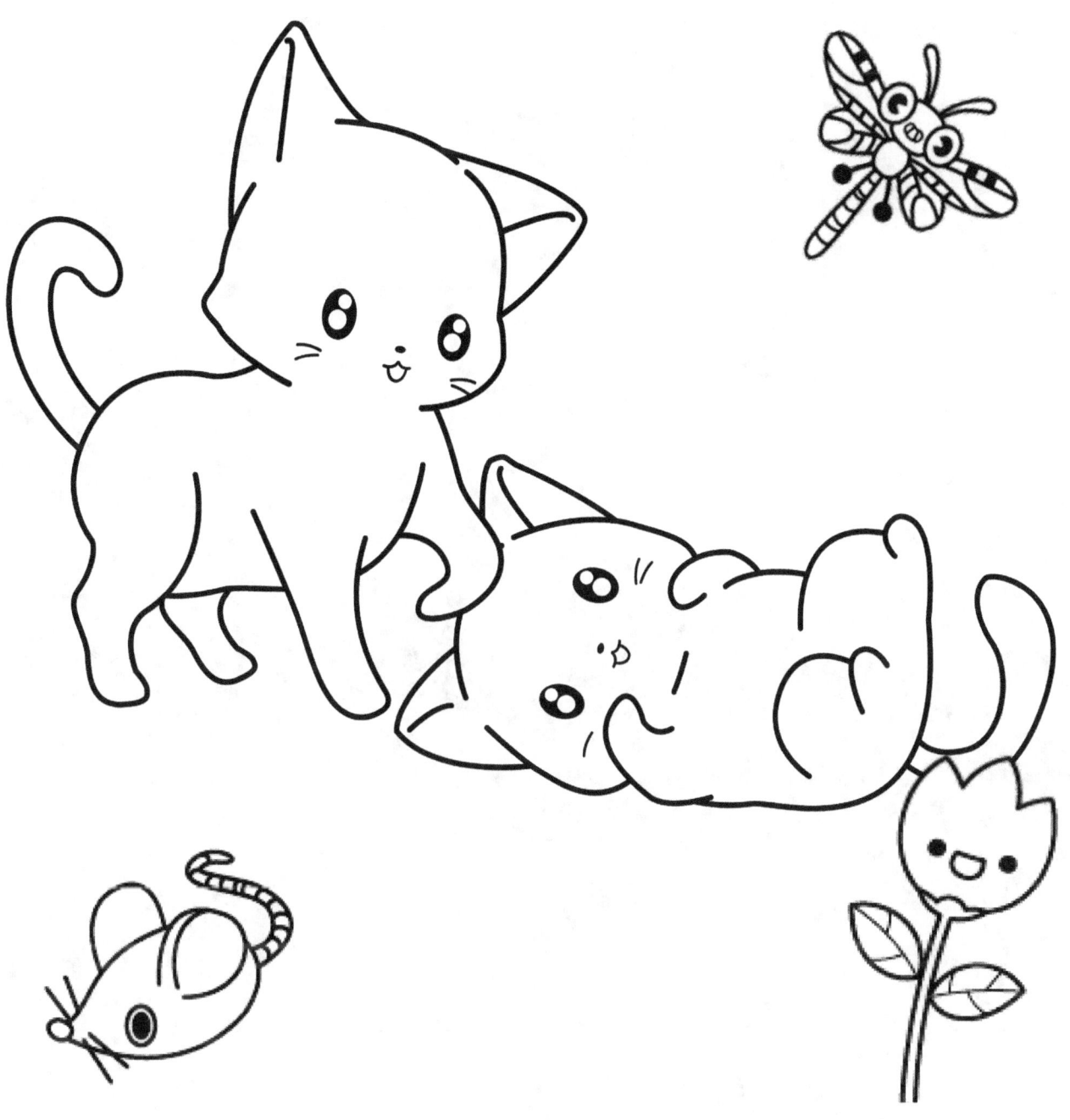

# My Magical Friends

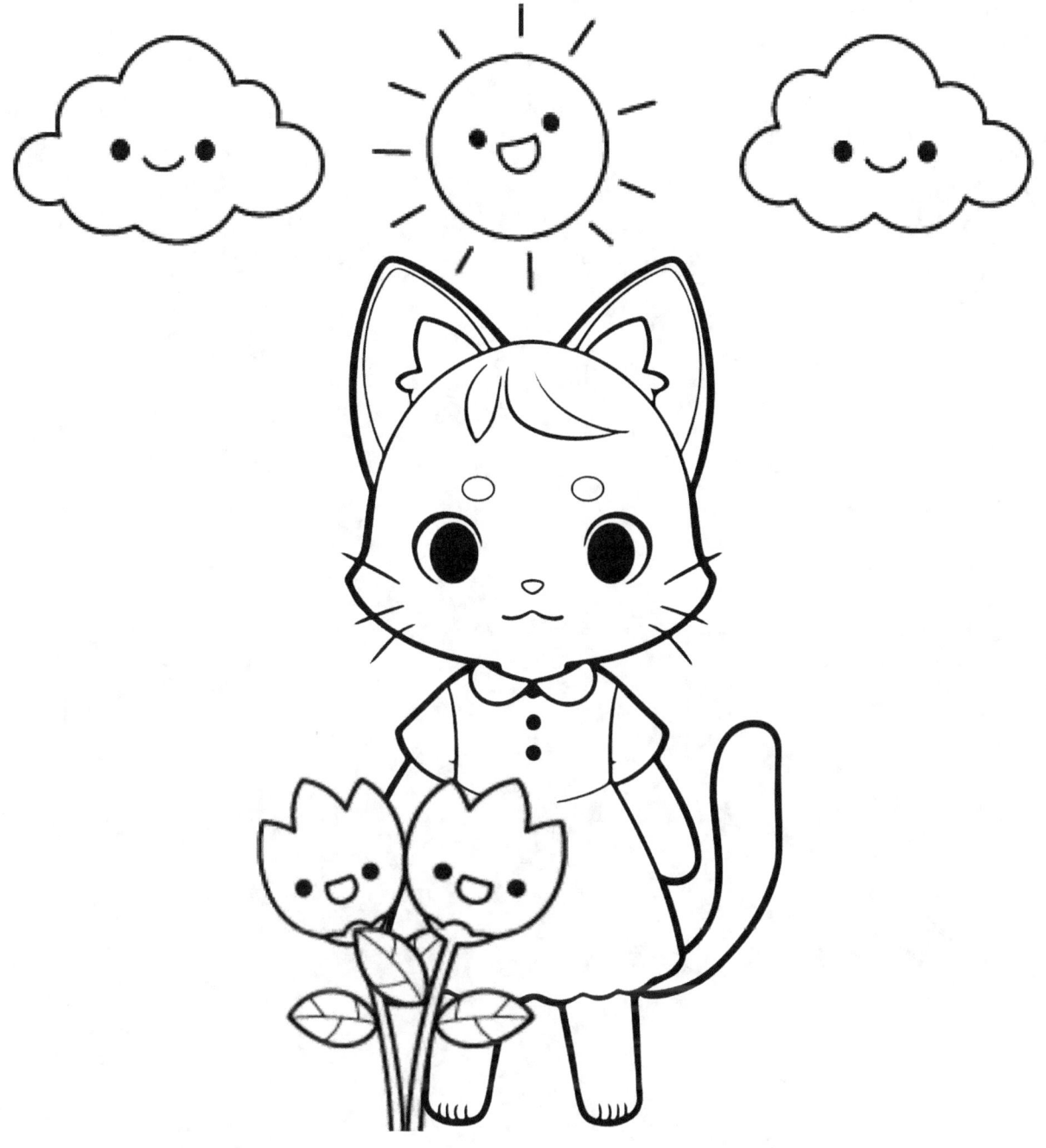

# Happiness on the way

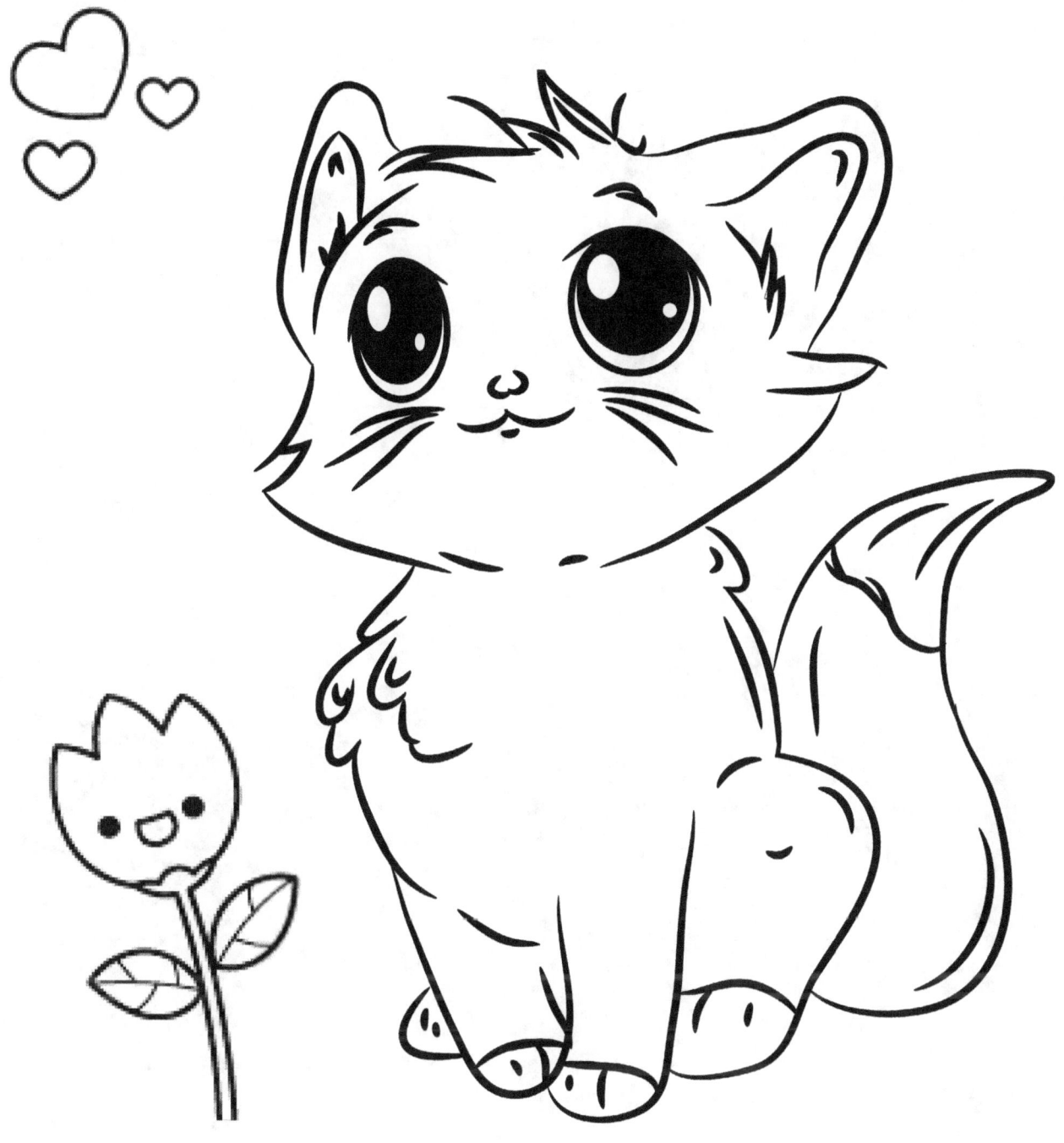

# Tell me something funny

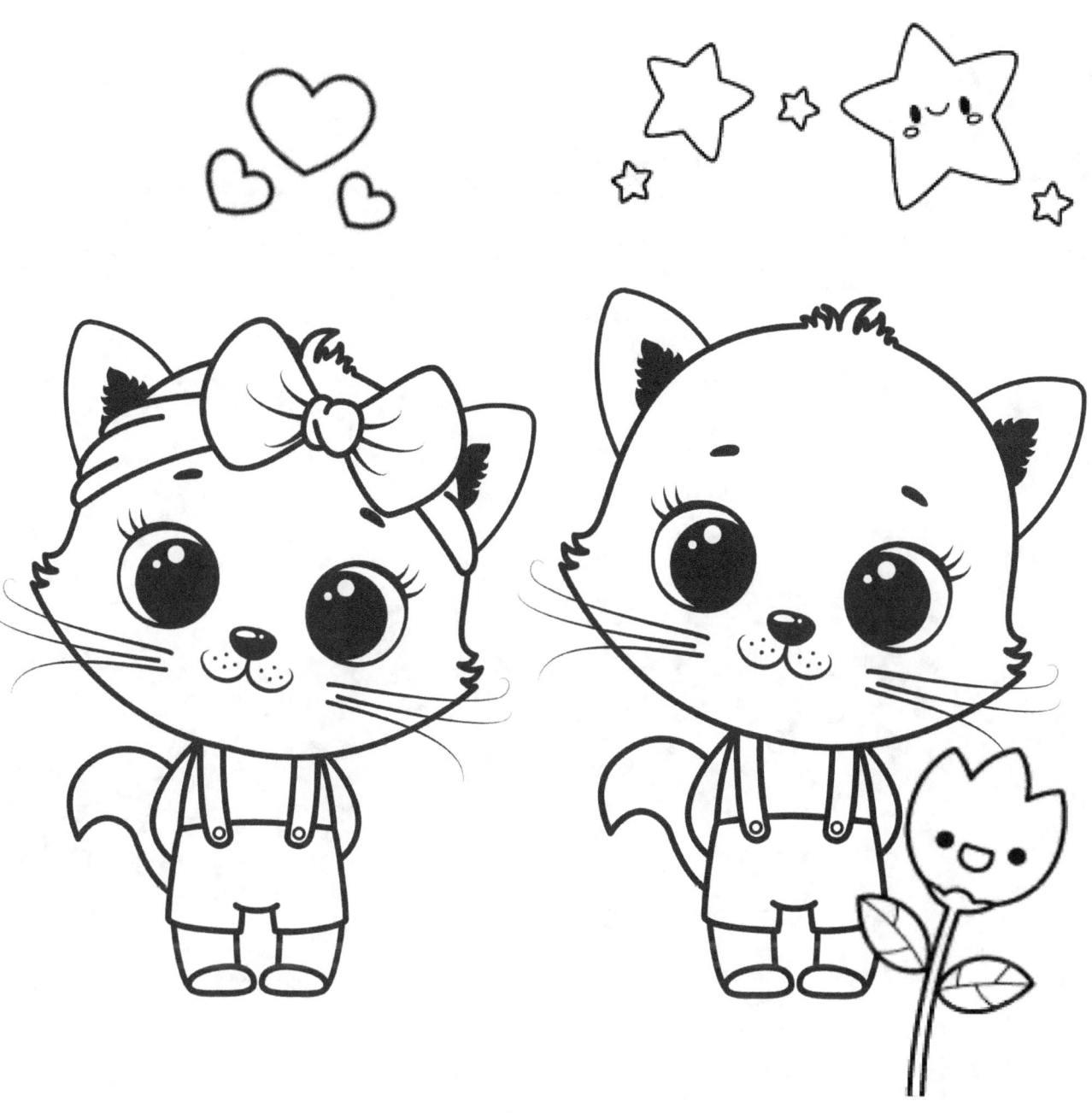

# Pure beauty

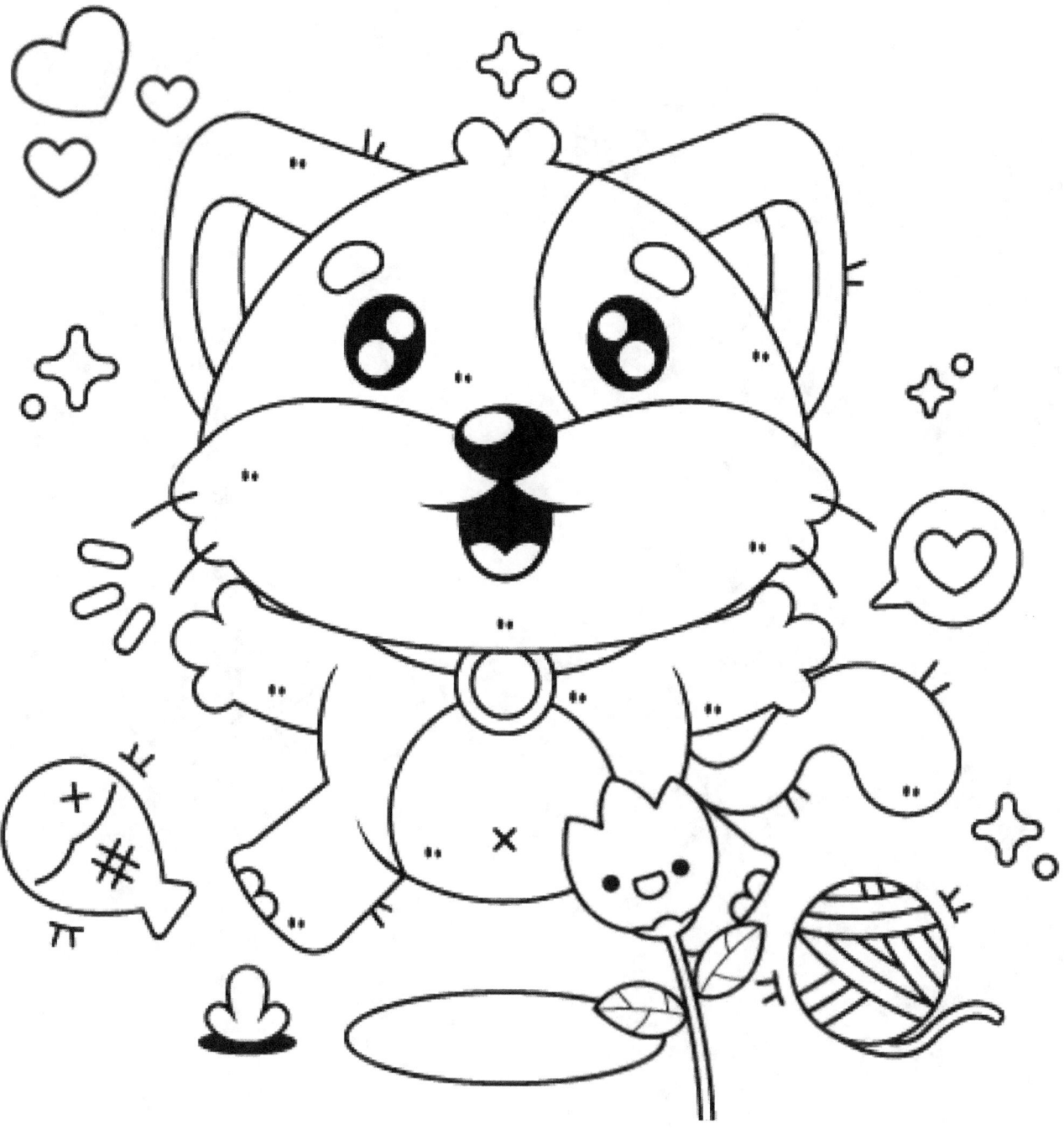

# Rest with joy

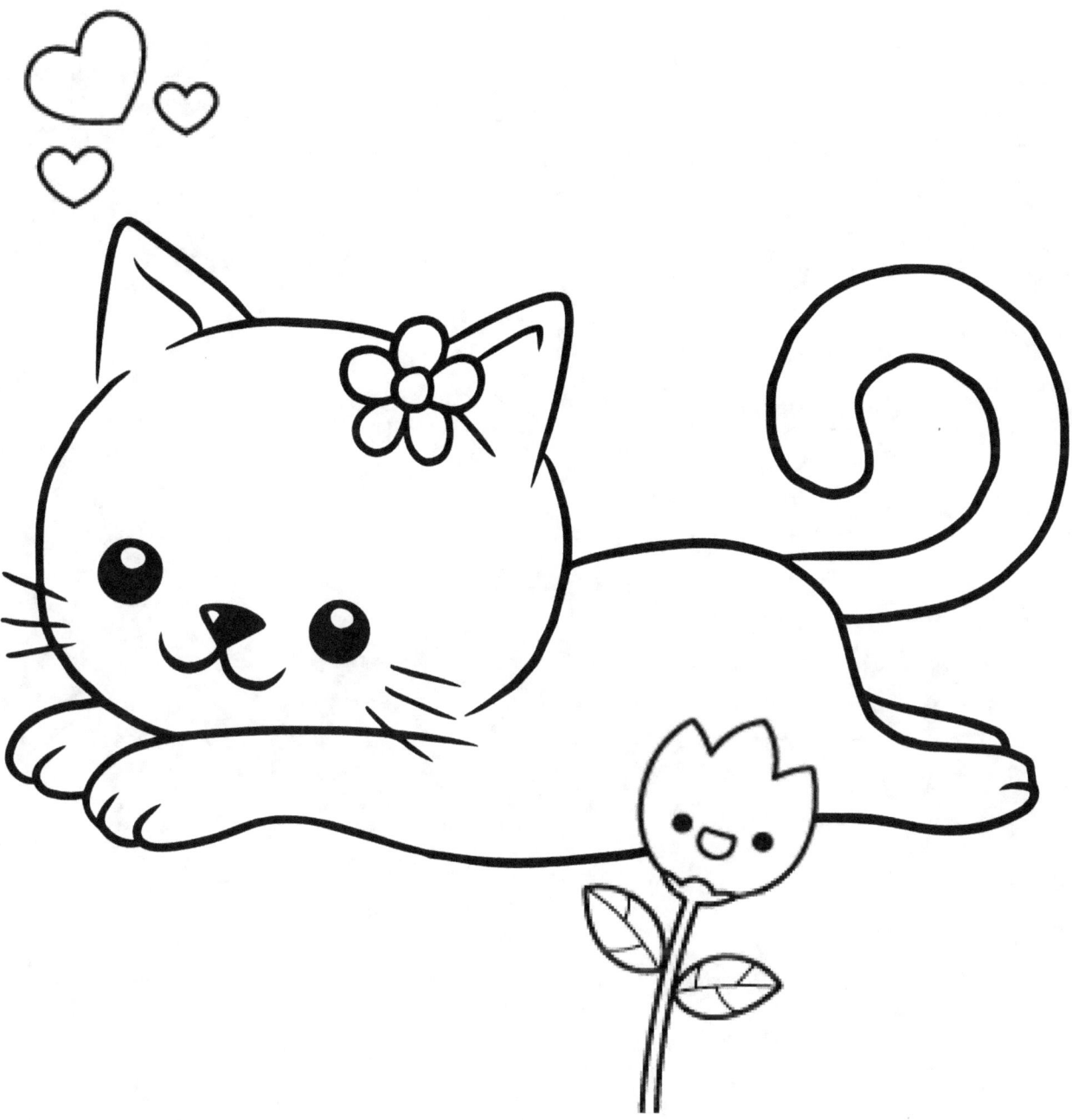

# A Kitten is a Warm
# Hug in the Form of Sound

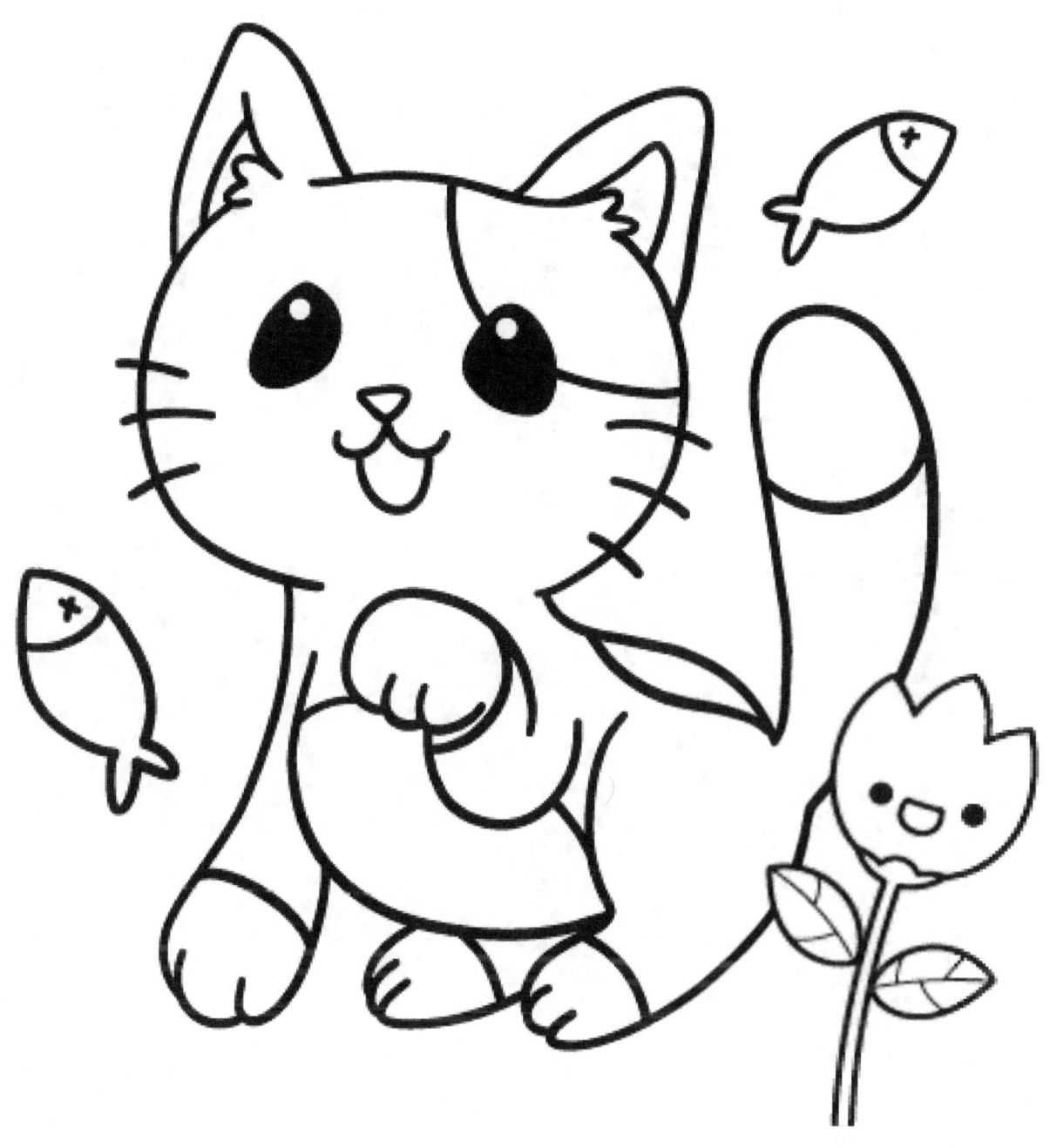

# Make a wish

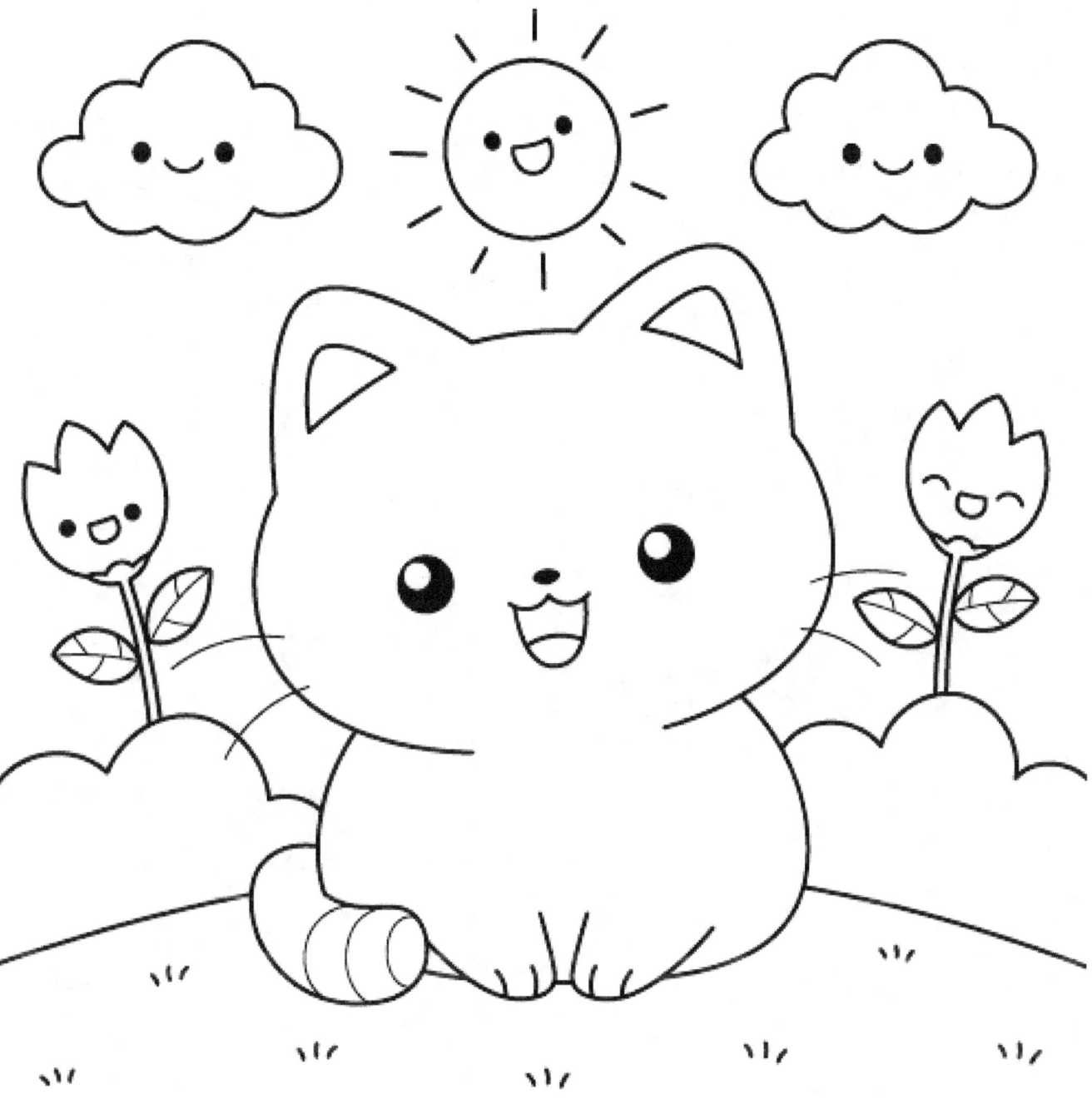

# A Gift with Love

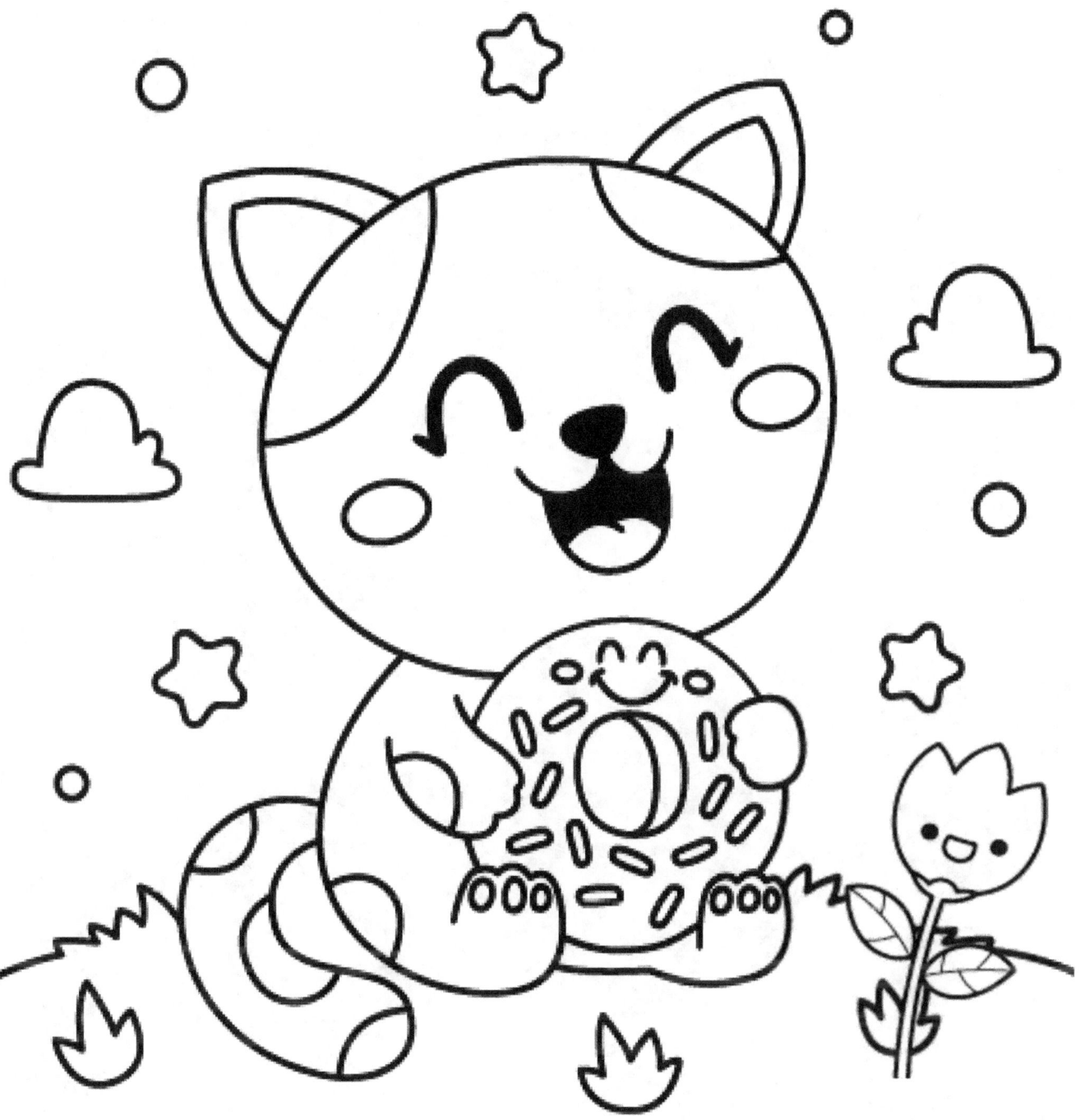

# Enjoy your day

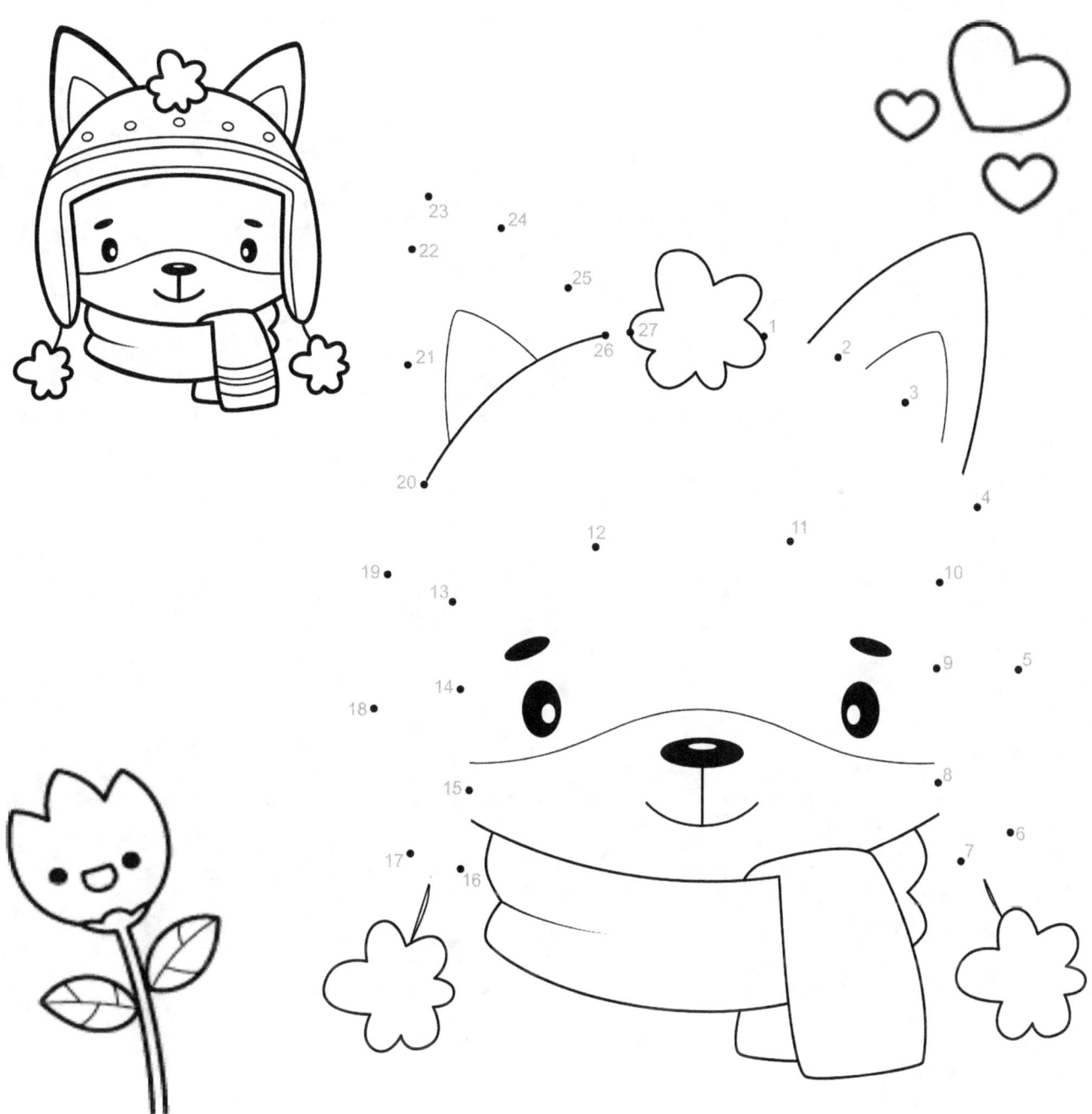

# Kittens invite you
# To Dream Without Limits

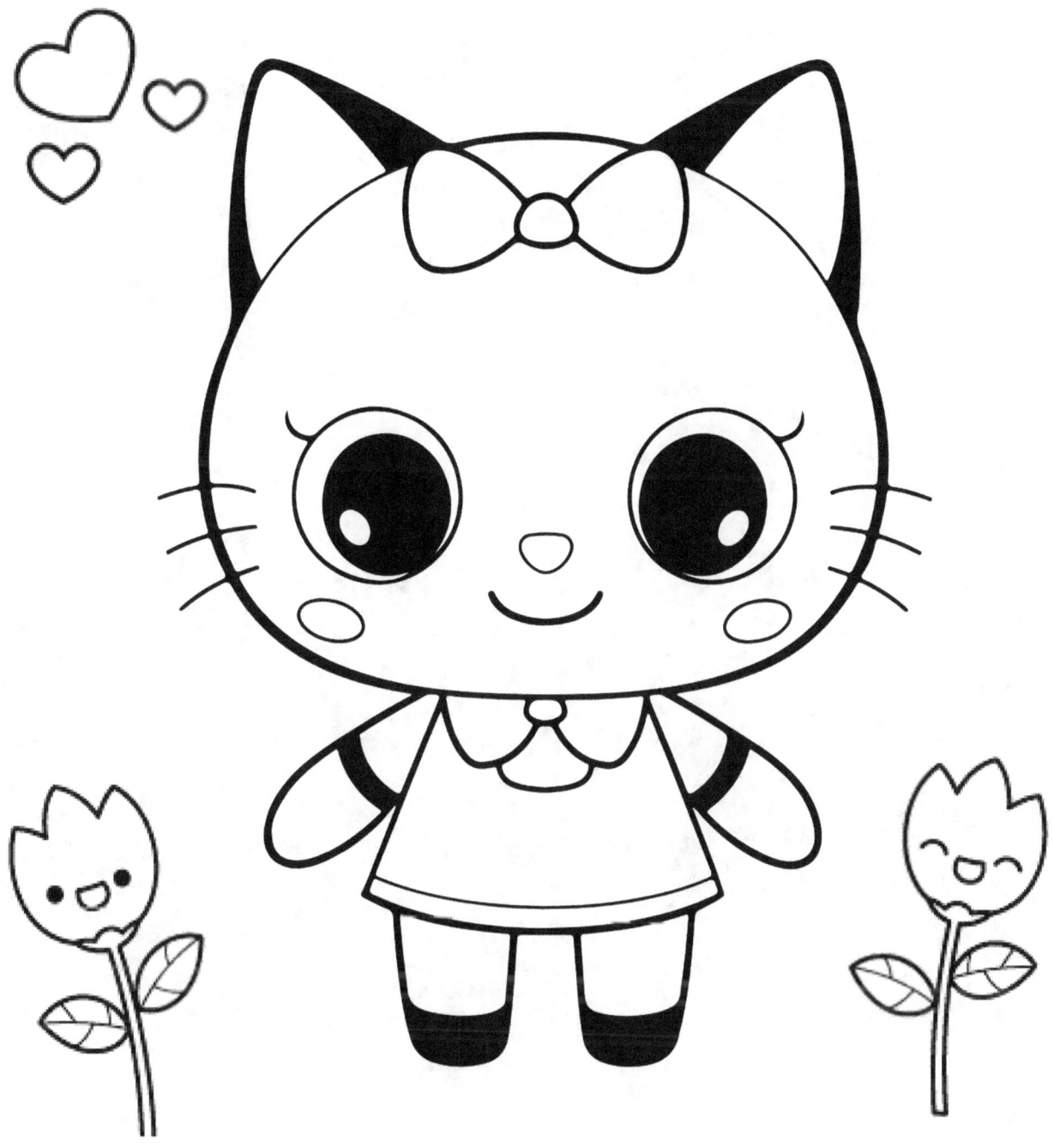

# A cat is a soft Heat
# Blanket That Covers The Heart

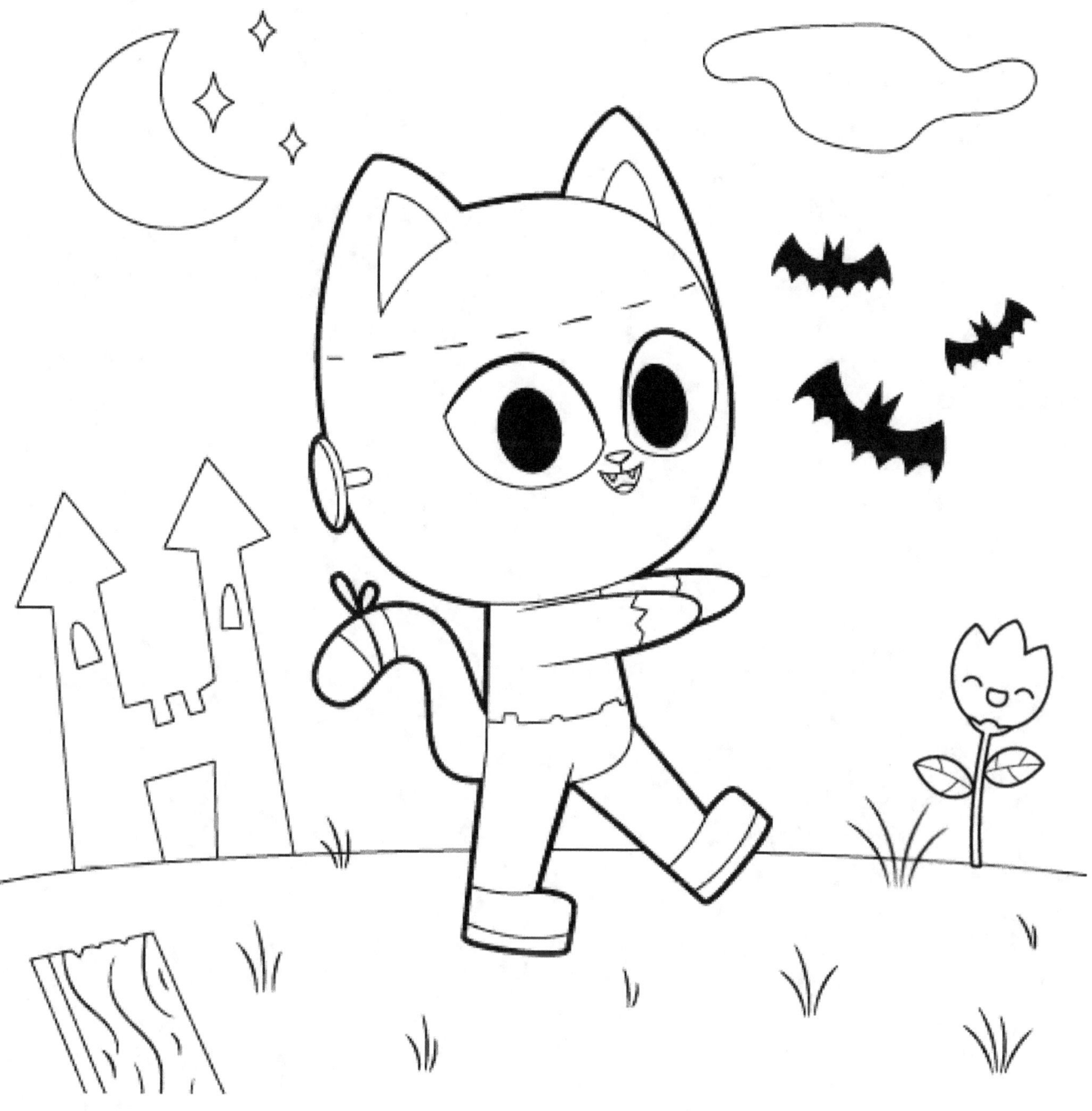

# Heart Bubbles

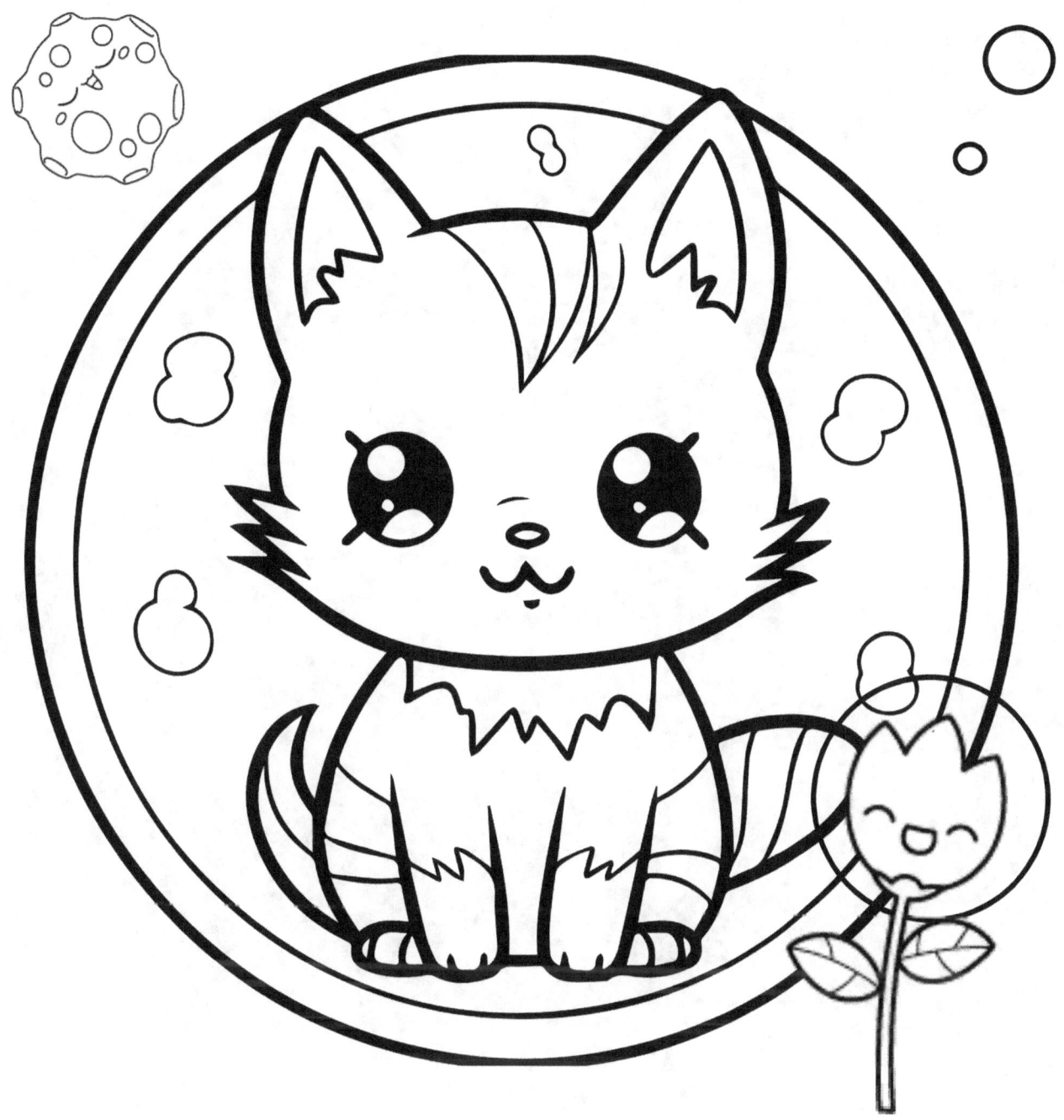

# Exploring the sky

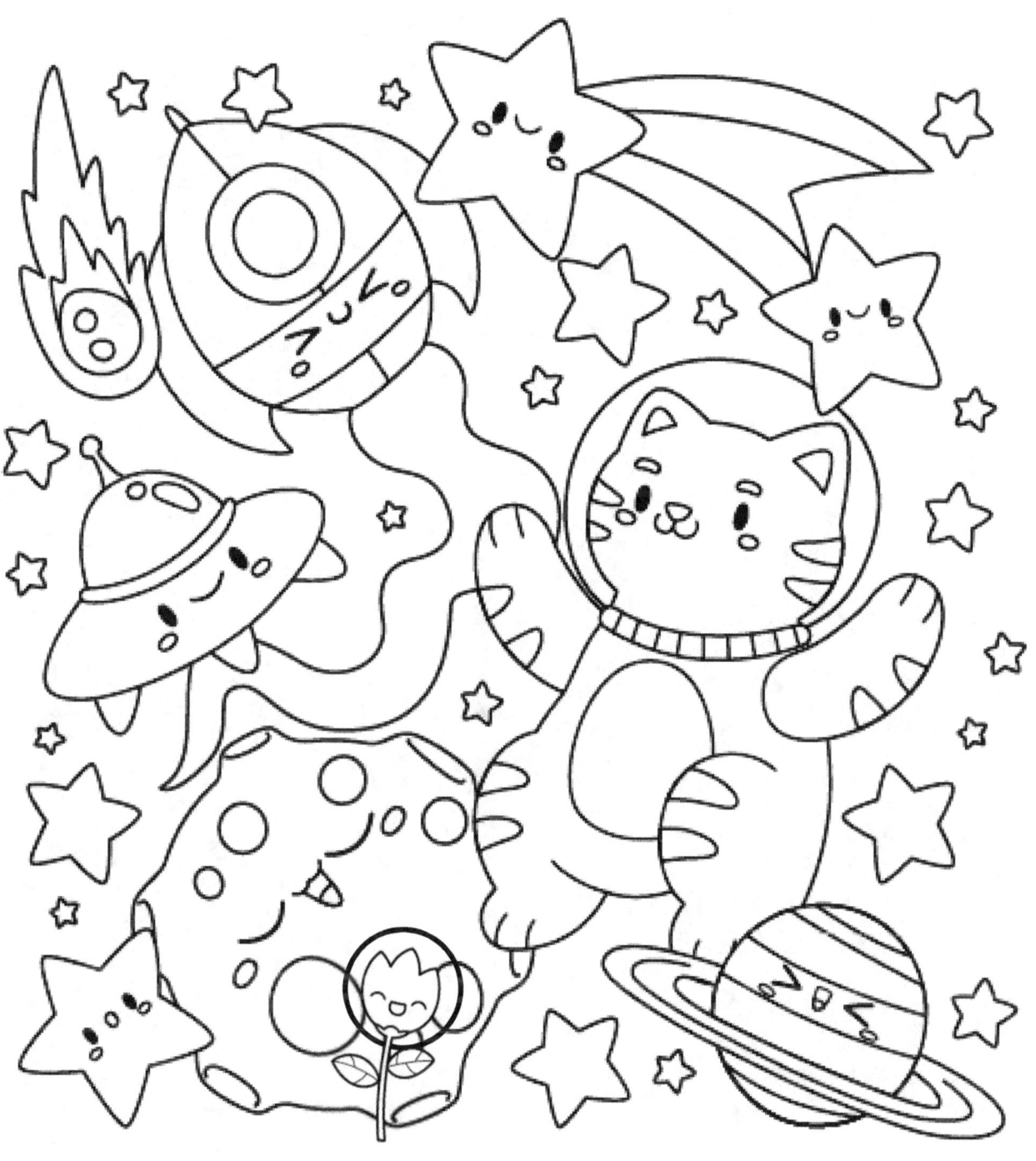

# At the end of the rainbow

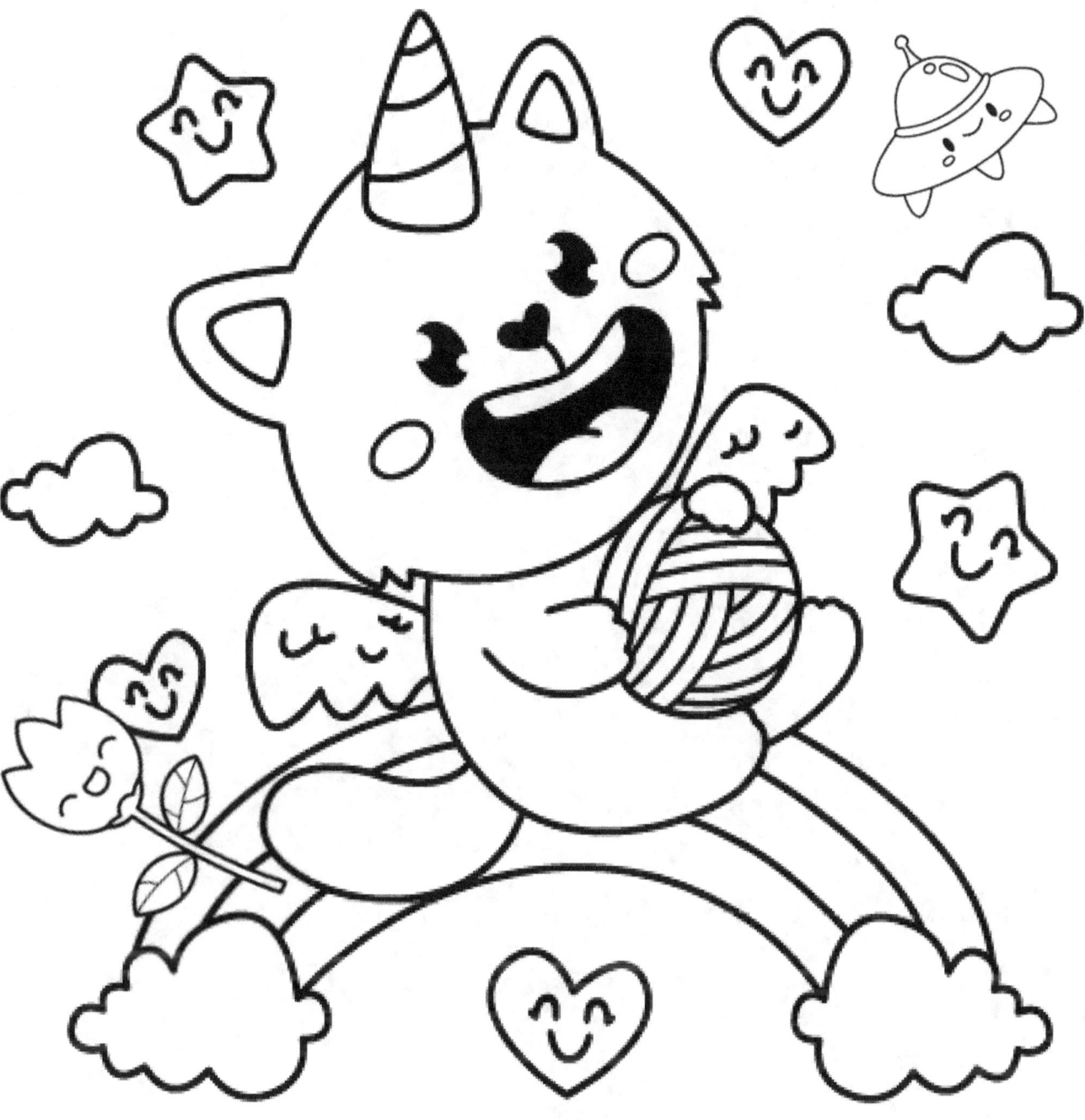

# Celebration
# Full of Smiles

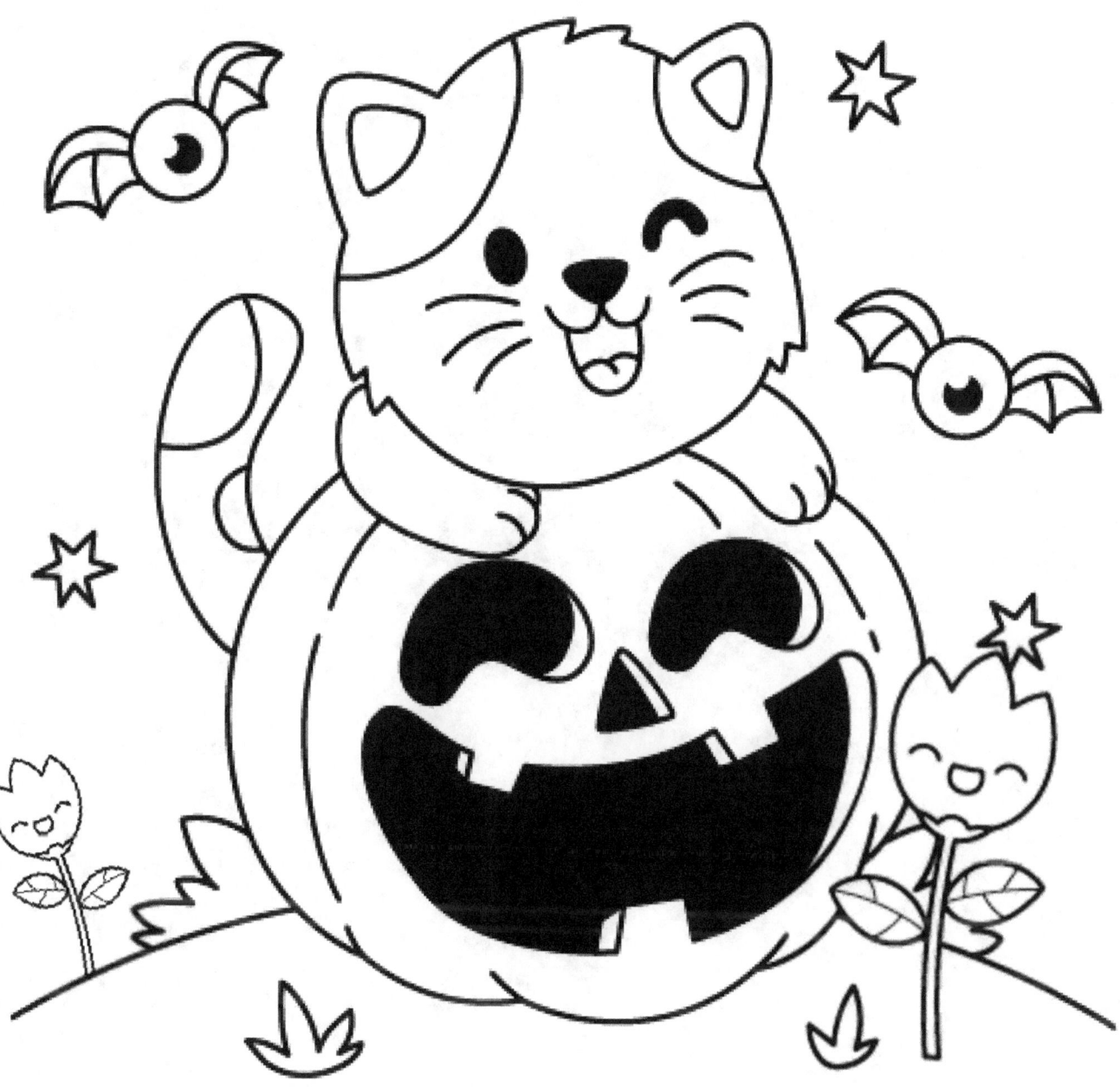

# Smile

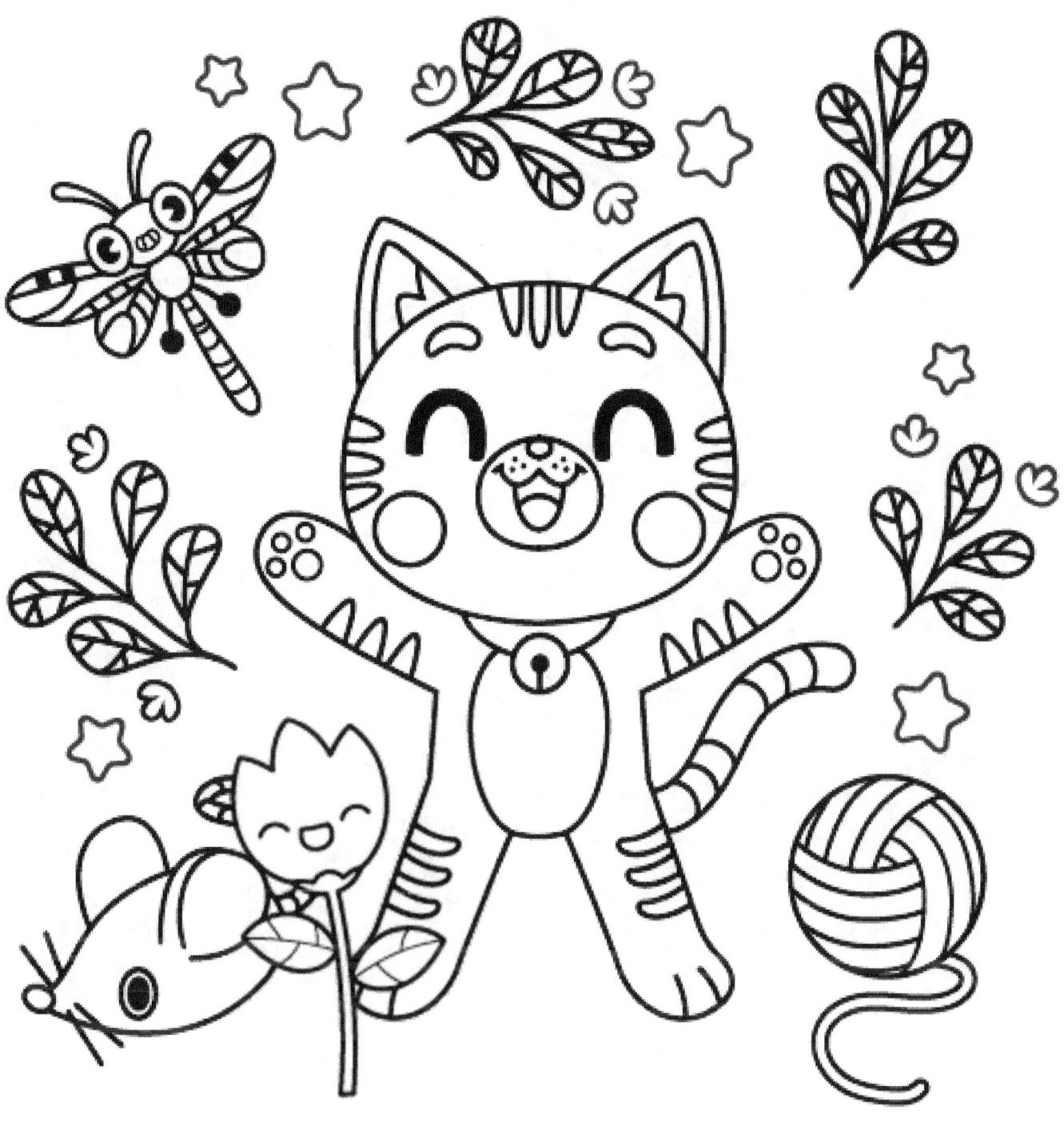

# Kittens are Real
## Princes and princesses

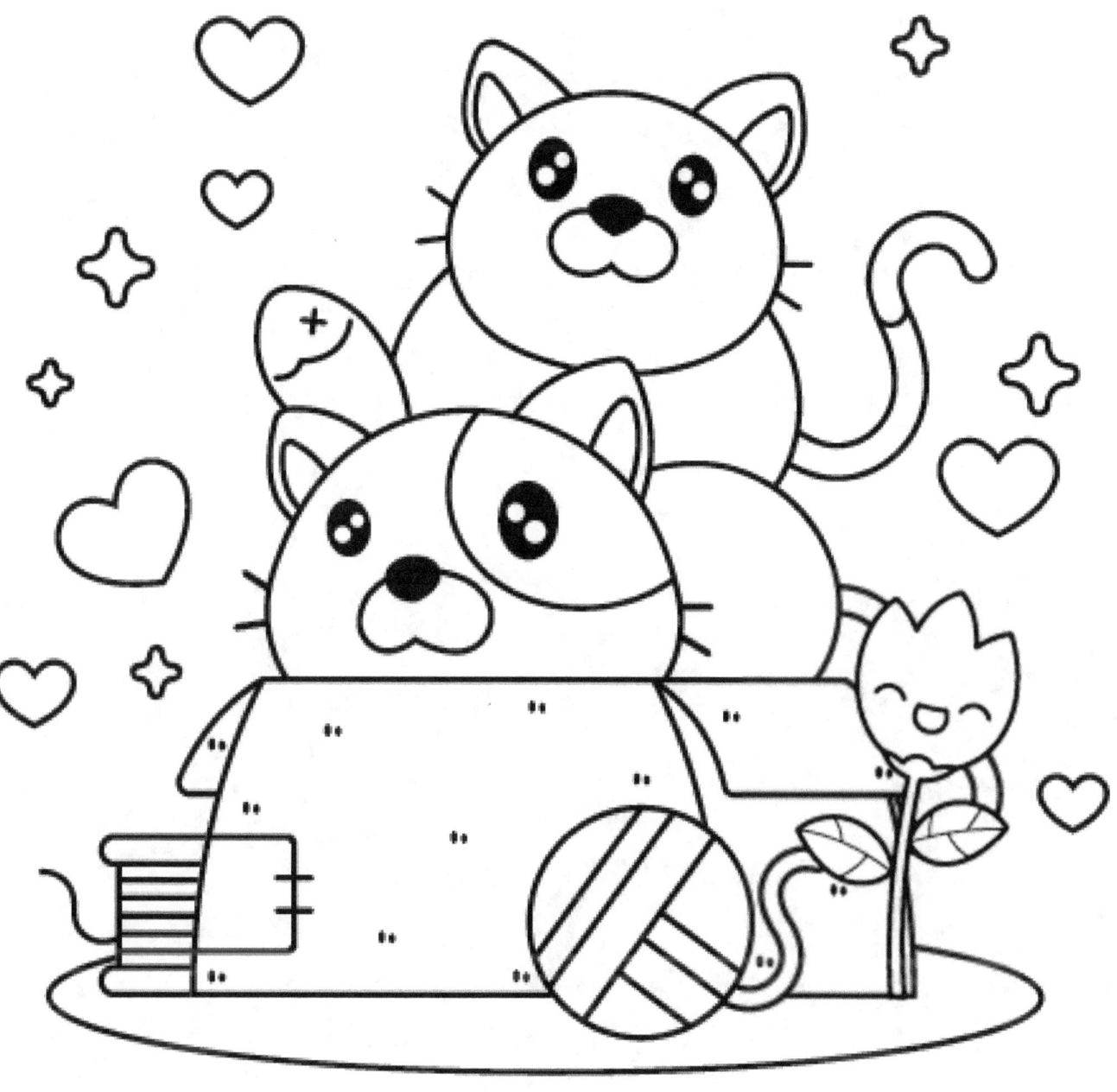

# Cats Purr Softly, Looking for Love and Company

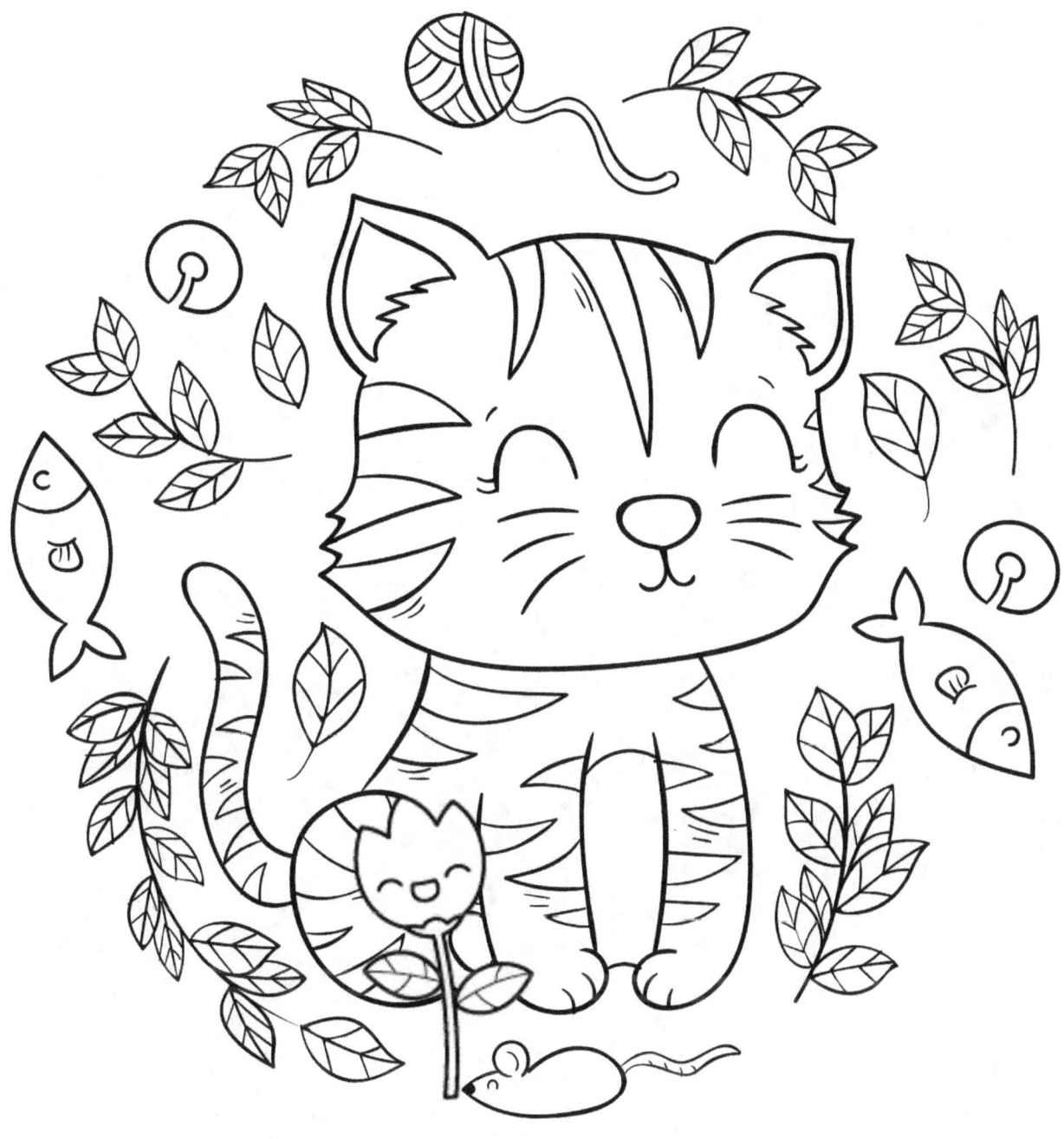

# The world stops for a Magical Moment

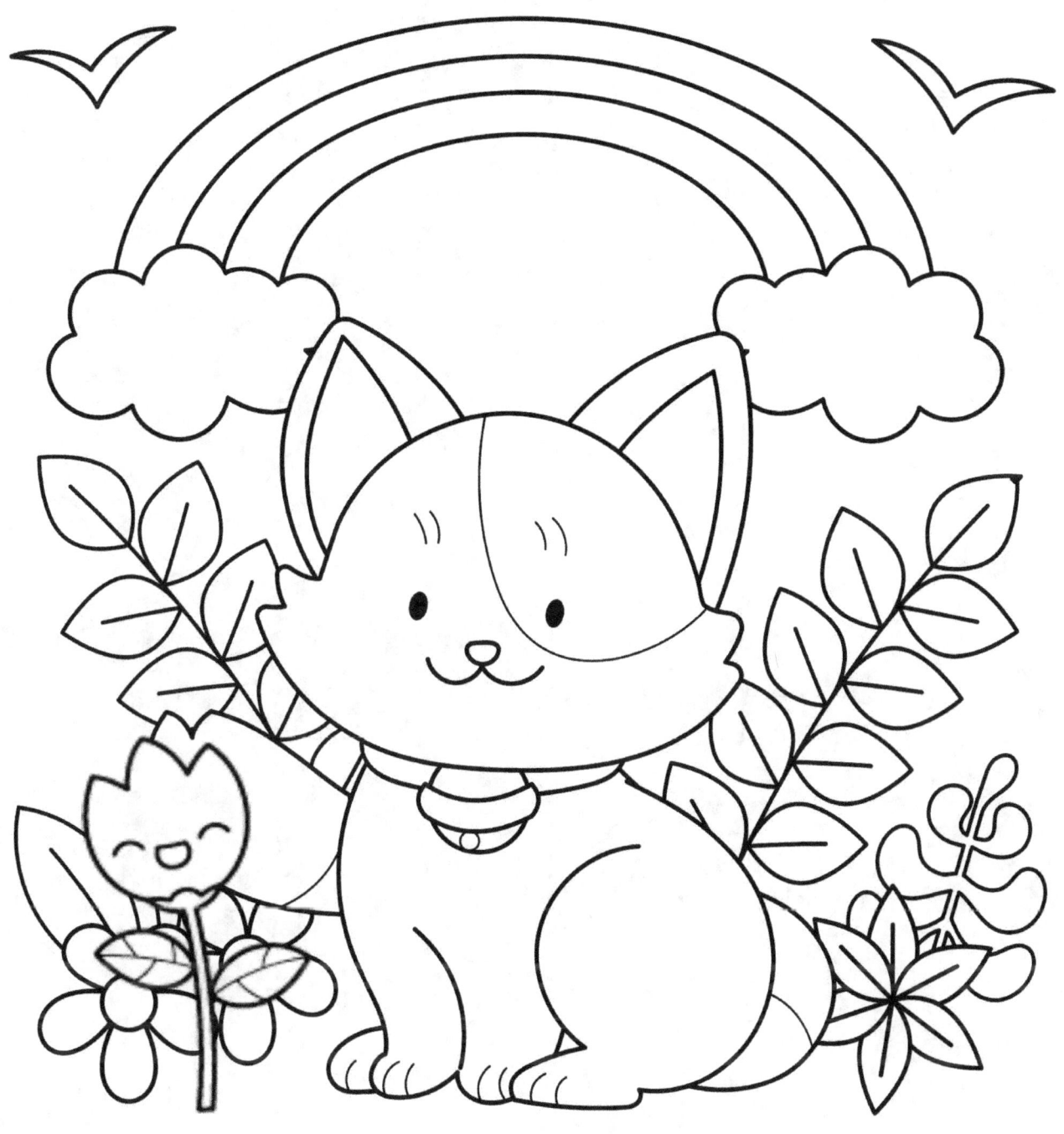

www.ingramcontent.com/pod-product-compliance
Lightning Source LLC
Chambersburg PA
CBHW081655220526
45466CB00009B/2771